For

_____

With love from

_____

Date

_____

*T*hus the heavens and the earth were completed in all their vast array.

GENESIS 2:1

You are part of something truly amazing.
Long, long ago, the world was a dark and dreary place.
But then God said four marvelous words:
"Let there be light."
This book is about what happened then.
As you'll see, God got very busy creating wondrous things.
And eventually, God said, "Let there be you."
God wanted you to shine your own special light of love, because
without you the world would not be quite as bright and beautiful.

God bless you,

Desmond Tutu

God's world is magical and magnificent.
God has put color everywhere!
As you explore the pictures in this book,
look for it in unexpected places.
I'll bet you'll find it!

And, as you grow up, I hope you'll not only
look for all the color in our beautiful world,
but also for all the love that has been added to it.

God has put love into everything in creation …
especially you!

Nancy Tillman

Nancy Tillman

William Collins
An imprint of HarperCollins*Publishers*
77–85 Fulham Palace Road,
Hammersmith, London W6 8JB
WilliamCollinsBooks.com

First published in Great Britain by William Collins in 2014

Published by arrangement with The Zondervan Corporation L.L.C.,
a subsidiary of HarperCollins Christian Publishing, Inc.

Text taken from *The Children of God Storybook Bible*, originally published in 2010 by
Lux Verbi, an imprint of NB Publishers, a division of Media24 (Boeke) Pty Ltd. Used with
permission

All Scripture quotations, unless otherwise indicated, are taken from the Holy Bible, *New
International Version®*, *NIV®*, Copyright© 1973, 1978, 1984, 2011 by Biblica, Inc.™ Used by
permission. All rights reserved worldwide.

A catalogue record for this book
is available from the British Library

ISBN 978-0-00-755258-0

Printed and bound in China

Editor: Barbara Herndon
Art direction and design: Kris Nelson

Let There Be Light

The Story of Creation
Retold by

Archbishop Desmond Tutu

Illustrated by *New York Times* bestselling author of *On the Night You Were Born*

Nancy Tillman

*I*n the very beginning, God's love bubbled over when there was nothing else—no trees, no birds, no animals, no sky, no sea— only darkness. Out of this love, God spoke.

"Let there be ligh

And there was day.

And there was night.

And when the first day
was done, God smiled
and knew that it was good.

On the second day, God said,
"Let there be sky where the clouds can
float and the wind can blow."

And the sky was bright blue and beautiful.

On the third day, God said,
"Let the waters gather
together into oceans and
let the dry land appear."

Now God decided to make the world even more dazzling, with tall trees and long grass.

And then the first flower opened in all its glory.

On the fourth day, God said,
"Let the sky be filled with
the sun and the moon."

And God scattered stars
across the sky like
sparkling diamonds.

On the fifth day, God said,
"Let there be birds to fly and sing,
and fish to swim and splash."

And the world was filled with the joyous
sound of birdsong.

On the sixth day, God said,
"Let there be animals—
elephants and giraffes ...

cats and mice ...

and bees and bugs."

And suddenly the world was a very noisy place.

But something was still missing.

Then God said,
"I will make people, and
I'll make them like me so
they can enjoy the earth
and take care of it."

He did just as he had
said, and it was all so
very, very good.

God looked at everything that he had made and clapped his hands together in delight.
"Isn't it wonderful!"

And on the seventh day, God laughed, and rested, and enjoyed his glorious creation.

You are loved.